RENEE WRIGHT

Hidden Havens for Retirees

Seven States That Offer More for Less in Your Golden Year

This book was professionally typeset on Reedsy.
Find out more at reedsy.com

Contents

Introduction

Think about retiring. For many Americans, it meant golden years full of laughter from grandchildren, coffee on the front porch in the morning, and the freedom to finally follow long-held dreams. But what does it mean to retire in the middle class in the United States today?

According to current standards, a middle-class person can retire with between $250,000 and $750,000 saved and monthly Social Security benefits of about $1,500 to $3,000. It means being able to live a simple but comfortable life, like owning or renting a good home, being able to pay for basic medical care, having some fun, and having some money saved up in case something comes up.

But middle-class retirees today face problems their parents never thought of. Healthcare costs have gone through the roof; the average 65-year-old couple might need $315,000 just for medical bills. Since many people switched from pensions to 401(k)s, they have to make difficult investment decisions on their own. At the same time, inflation hurts fixed incomes, and traditional places to retire are getting more and more expensive.

Because of this, we used a method that goes beyond typical "best places" lists to do a full analysis of retirement-friendly states. For eighteen months, our research team looked at data from a number of different sources, such as:

- U.S. Census Bureau economic and demographic data
- Tax records from the state and city

- Metrics for healthcare accessibility
- Indicators of the cost of living
- Numbers about climate change and natural disasters
- Data on crime and safety
- The availability of social and cultural amenities

Most importantly, we talked to hundreds of middle-class retirees who were able to move and learned from both their successes and failures. Their real-life experiences helped us find states where middle-income budgets really work.

Several important factors were given weight to our analysis:

- The cost of housing (30% of the total score)
- Access to and quality of healthcare (25%) 15% of retirement income is taxed.
- Cost of living other than housing (10%)
- Risk of climate change and natural disasters (10%)
- Amenities for social and cultural life (5%)
- Crime rates and safety (5%)

We came to some surprising conclusions thanks to this methodical approach. Some traditional places to retire were on our list, but others were too pricey for middle-class people to afford. At the same time, a number of unexpected states emerged as hidden gems, offering unique mixes of low costs and high quality of life.

In this book the best retirement options for middle-class people are laid out. You can use it to plan your own retirement or help a loved one make this important choice. Because living in the right place can turn your retirement from a constant struggle with money into the wonderful time of your life it's meant to be.

Let's start our search for the perfect place for you to retire.

1

Florida: A New Look at an Old Favorite

When you say "retirement in Florida," most people think of expensive condos on the beach in Miami or high-end communities in Naples. But Florida today has a lot more to offer than these high-end spots. Middle-class retirees who are smart are finding a new side of the Sunshine State that is affordable and still has all the benefits that have made Florida a popular place to retire for generations.

This is why Florida is on the list:

The real game changer is the state income tax of zero.

```
Not having a state income tax in Florida isn't just a small perk;
it's a huge help to your retirement budget.
```

This amounts to the following in real money:

- Social Security benefits are not taxed.
- Pension income stays in your pocket.
- Withdrawals from an IRA or 401(k) are not taxed at the state level.
- And only federal taxes are applied to investment income.

This could mean that a middle-class retiree with $40,000 a year in retirement income gets to keep an extra $2,000 to $3,000 a year instead of having to pay income tax.

Homestead Exemption: Your Safety Net for Money

One of the best homestead exemptions in the country is in Florida:

- You don't have to pay property taxes on the first $50,000 of your home's value (except for school district taxes).
- Assessments on primary residences will go up by no more than 3% each year. Your primary residence will be protected from creditors.
- People whose spouses have died may be able to get more exemptions

What is the real value?

If you buy a $250,000 home in Florida instead of many other states, you might save $1,000 or more a year on property taxes.

Low-Cost Coastal Living: Hidden Gems Not in the Spotlight

While Miami Beach and Naples get all the attention, these less expensive coastal towns offer similar lifestyles at a much lower cost.

1. Port Charlotte: The average price of a home is about $275,000
2. New Smyrna Beach is a quiet beach town where prices are 40% less than in nearby Daytona
3. Old Florida charm in Fort Pierce, where the average home price is less than $250,000

4. Panama City has easy access to the Gulf and reasonable home prices

Tip: Look for homes that are 5 to 10 miles inland from the coast. Prices often drop by 30 to 40 percent, and you can still easily get to the beach.

All Year The Weather is More than Just Warm

Florida's weather has some special benefits:

Weather in the winter is usually between 61°F and 70°F, and there are about 237 sunny days a year.

- You don't need to buy expensive winter clothes or tools to clear the snow.
- Longer outdoor season means less money spent on entertainment
- Lower heating costs than northern states

But smart retirees should think about:

- Higher cooling costs in the summer (June to September);
- The need for hurricane insurance;
- The need for reliable air conditioning
- The importance of getting ready for storms

There are many good things about Florida, but to make the right choice, you need to think about more than just taxes and weather. To have a successful retirement in Florida, you should know all about your healthcare options, carefully look at how much it really costs to live, and find a community that fits your budget and way of life. Let's look more closely at these important points to help you decide if and where Florida might be the best place for you to retire.

Things to Think About

If you want to retire in Florida, you need to carefully consider three important factors that can make or break your experience: the cost of living, the ease of getting medical care, and how well the state prepares for storms. The Sunshine State has great infrastructure and medical care, but it's important to know what insurance you need and how to prepare for bad weather. Let's look at these important factors that will affect your daily life and your happiness with your choice to retire in Florida in the long term.

Infrastructure for Health Care

Because Florida is known as a great place to retire, it has one of the best healthcare systems in the country for seniors. The state has some of the best medical care in the country, with world-class hospitals and special programs for caring for seniors.

The Mayo Clinic in Jacksonville and the Cleveland Clinic in Weston are two well-known hospitals that are at the heart of Florida's health care system. These anchor a network of over 300 hospitals statewide, with major concentrations in Tampa/St. Petersburg (22 facilities), Orlando (15 hospitals), and Miami-Dade County (25+ facilities). These facilities are strategically placed so that most residents can get to an emergency room within 20 minutes. This is especially helpful for retirees.

It's not just hospitals, though. The state of Florida has built a complex system for caring for seniors which includes:

— **Specialized Treatment Centers:**
  *15 cancer centers ranked in the top 15 in the country
  * 22 cardiac care specialty centers
  * 35+ orthopedic specialty clinics
  * 28 memory disorder clinics

Florida has creative healthcare options for seniors that are made to meet their day-to-day needs. Even though they cost between $1,500 and $3,000 a year, concierge medical practices make it easier to get in touch with doctors and give more personalized care. Medicare Advantage HMO plans are widely accepted, and many places have doctors who will come to your home, which is helpful for people who have trouble moving around.

Things to Think About for Hurricanes and Storms

If you live in Florida, you have to be ready for hurricane season. From June to November, people need to pay attention to the weather and make sure they are ready for anything. This may sound scary, but Florida has some of the world's most advanced emergency management systems, and if you're ready, you'll be much less likely to be hurt.

It's important to know what insurance requirements are needed:

- **Needs for Policy Coverage:**

  • Basic homeowner's insurance: $1,500 to $2,500 a year;
  • Hurricane coverage: an extra $800 to $1,500 a year;
  • Flood insurance: $600-$2,500 a year, depending on location;
  • Wind damage coverage: usually needs a separate policy.

Smart homeowners can cut their insurance costs by a large amount by making some changes to their homes. If you install impact windows, your insurance rates may go down by 15%, and if you install hurricane shutters, they may go down by 5 to 15%. Your rates can go down by 5 to 10 percent just by picking a house with a hip roof.

Prepare for a storm in more ways than one. Everyone who lives in Florida should keep up with:

- Essentials for an emergency kit:

- A week's worth of water (1 gallon per person per day);
- Food that won't go bad for seven days;
- A battery-powered weather radio;
- External chargers for electronics;
- A waterproof container for important papers;
- Prescription drugs and first aid supplies

Most importantly, you need a plan for getting out of the building. Not only should you know the fastest way to get inland, but you should also have a full plan that includes:

—A clear idea of where your evacuation zone is:

- Two main and two backup evacuation routes
- Plans for getting pets out of the area if needed
- Copies of important documents ready to go
- Registering your special needs with your county if needed

Tip: When looking for a house, look at maps of flood zones and elevations. Where your home is in these zones can have a big effect on your insurance rates and how you have to evacuate.

Cost Analysis and Lifestyle Advantages

Florida is appealing to middle-class retirees because it strikes a good balance between cost of living and quality of life. To make an informed decision, you need to know how much it really costs to live in Florida while also looking into the state's many lifestyle options.

Markets for Homes Under $250,000

Even if you can't afford a home on the beach, Florida has a lot of affordable homes in nice neighborhoods. Most homes in Ocala, which is known for its horse farms and rolling hills, cost around $225,000. Homes in Spring Hill cost an average of $240,000. The neighborhood is great for families and is close to the Gulf Coast. Port St. Lucie is a growing city on the coast, but homes there still start at $245,000. In Lakeland, on the other hand, homes in the charming historic district with views of the lake often cost less than $230,000.

Communities that aren't as well known have even better deals. Consider Marion Oaks or Palm Bay. In those areas, well-kept homes can be bought for less than $200,000, and lots are available for around $220,000. These places might not look like they belong in vacation guides, but they are nice places to live and have all the amenities you could want.

Insurance Things to Think About

Florida's insurance landscape needs to be carefully negotiated. Besides the hurricane coverage we already talked about, you'll also need to plan for:

- Home insurance rates vary by region; coastal areas usually pay 30–40% more.
- Auto insurance costs about $1,200 a year in rural areas and $1,800 a year in cities.
- Health insurance plans that cover extra costs (plan for $150 to $300 a month)
- Options for long-term care insurance (starting at about $200 a month at age 65)
- Umbrella policies cost $200 to $400 a year and offer extra liability protection.

Costs of utilities

The weather in Florida has a direct effect on your monthly bills. In a typical 2,000-square-foot home, you can expect the following:

- Electricity costs $150 to $225 (much more in the summer).
- Water: $40 to $70 (more if you take care of a lawn)
- Internet and cable: $80 to $120
- Natural gas or propane: $30 to $50 (if needed)
- Trash Pickup: $20 to $35
- Other things to think about are pool maintenance ($80–$150 a month) and lawn care ($60–$100 a month).

Lifestyle Pros and Cons

Active Communities for Adults

Florida's 55+ communities have changed over time to offer a wider range of lifestyle choices at a range of prices. The best neighborhoods have places to hang out with other people and features that encourage people to live active lives. Most of them offer:

- Fitness centers and pools for the community
- Set up clubs and social activities
- Gated entrances and security features
- Repair and maintenance services
- There are walking paths and sports courts.

In more expensive neighborhoods, there may be golf courses, tennis courts, and resort-style features. But keep in mind that more features mean higher monthly fees. A lot of retirees think that mid-tier communities are the best value because they have a lot to do without costing too much.

Opportunities for outdoor recreation

Florida is more than just its famous beaches—it's a natural playground.
- 663 miles of beaches where you can swim, walk, and collect shells
- 7,800 lakes where you can fish, boat, and kayak;

- 175 state parks where you can camp, hike, and watch birds;
- More than 1,300 golf courses, many with senior discounts at twilight hours
- Huge networks of bike paths, including rails-to-trails

The weather in the state makes outdoor activities possible all year, but smart retirees plan activities for early in the morning in the summer to avoid the hottest parts of the day.

Places of interest in culture

Many newcomers are surprised by how deep and varied Florida's cultural scene is:

There are museums with everything from world-class art collections to interesting local history displays, theater companies putting on Broadway hits and original works, music venues putting on everything from symphony orchestras to rock concerts, festivals all year long celebrating art, music, food, and local heritage, educational opportunities at community colleges and universities, and professional baseball, football, hockey, and basketball teams.

A lot of cities have discounts or special programs for seniors who live there. There are often free admission days at museums in St. Petersburg, and places like The Villages often have touring performers and lecturers.

```
Pro Tip: When exploring potential communities, ask about
reciprocal membership programs between cultural venues. A lot of
Florida's attractions are part of networks that let members use
more than one facility.
```

Often, the key to a happy retirement in Florida is picking a place that strikes a good balance between these factors based on your own needs. A neighborhood might have very cheap housing, but it might take longer to get to cultural attractions. Another might offer a lot of things to do, but the monthly fees might be higher. Before making a decision, take the time to visit during different times of the year, talk to people who already live there, and carefully weigh the costs and benefits.

> Remember that Florida is very big and has a lot of different things. If your first choice doesn't feel right after living there, many retirees find success by relocating within the state as they better understand their preferences and needs.

Many people think that retirement in Florida is the same for everyone, but it's not. Just ask Jim and Maria Wilson, who chose a cute town in central Florida over the expensive beach spots. "Everyone assumed we'd head straight to Naples or Boca Raton," Maria says with laughter. "In Mount Dora, we found our peaceful place." We have lakes, culture, and great health care, and it only costs half as much as we thought it would. And those expensive coastal towns? When we want them, they're only a day trip away.

To be successful in the middle class in Florida, you need to know where to look. While tourists and wealthy retirees flock to well-known destinations, savvy retirees are discovering vibrant communities like Venice, Winter Garden, and Dunedin. These hidden gems offer Florida's well-known benefits, like no state income tax, homestead exemptions, and the chance to live outside all year, but they don't cost as much as more well-known places.

Looking ahead, Florida's dedication to building up infrastructure and expanding healthcare will continue to help retirees from middle-class families.

Smaller towns are getting new medical facilities, transportation systems are getting better, and technology projects are making services better in places other than the big cities. Some areas have trouble with coastal property insurance, but communities inland are doing well and changing to meet the needs of retirees.

If you're thinking about retiring in Florida, here's an idea: see more of the state than just its postcards. To really understand the way of life, you should go during different times of the year, even summer. If you go inland from the coasts, you can find cute towns where your retirement funds will go further. To get a feel for daily life, talk to people in coffee shops, check out community centers, and go to events in your area.

For middle-class retirees, Florida isn't about fancy condos or private country clubs. It's about finding the places where prices are fair and quality of life is great. Florida still has a lot to offer middle-class retirees who want to do well, whether it's watching manatees from a nearby park, taking walks in the evening through historic neighborhoods, or going to cultural events without having to pay the high prices of big cities.

Even though you have a middle-class budget, the Sunshine State is still a good place to retire. It's important to know where to look, when to look, and how to tell the difference between retirement gold and tourist glitter. After all, the best way to retire in Florida isn't to follow the crowd to the most expensive spots; it's to be smart enough to find your own paradise that doesn't break the bank.

2

Tennessee: The Musical Haven for Retirees on a Budget

Tennessee is a surprising winner for middle-class retirees who want to make the most of their retirement money while still living a good life. Aside from tax breaks, the Volunteer State has quietly become one of the best places to retire because of its low cost of living and ability to help people save money. This is something that appears less common these days.

Tennessee's big tax breaks are what make the state so appealing. Many states take a big chunk out of retirees' income, but Tennessee is different because it doesn't tax salaries, wages, or retirement income. This means that the state will not tax your Social Security benefits, pension payments, or 401(k) distributions. This means that you can keep more of the money you've worked hard for. For retirees from the middle class, this tax break can mean saving thousands of dollars a year, which they can then use to enjoy life instead of paying bills.

The state is still committed to making sure retirees have enough money. Tennessee has some of the lowest property taxes in the country, and many counties give seniors extra breaks. This is especially important for retirees on fixed incomes because it makes long-term homeownership more likely.

Even better, these low property taxes apply to both small and large homes, so retirees can choose the best place to live for them without having to worry about paying too much in taxes.

Possibly most importantly, Tennessee has a moderate cost of living that makes it easy to afford daily life. Average costs for things like groceries and utilities are usually lower than the national average. Housing costs are also lower in many desirable areas than in coastal retirement havens, which is a big economic benefit. You can get more for your retirement money in Tennessee, whether you want a cozy condo in downtown Nashville or a quiet mountain cabin in the Smokies.

But the numbers aren't the only thing that makes Tennessee appealing. It's possible to retire here because of the money, but it's the state's rich culture, varied landscapes, and lively communities that make it truly desirable. Tennessee has a way of life that is just as good as any place to retire. From the blues clubs of Memphis to the country music halls of Nashville, and from the mountain trails of Gatlinburg to the cute main streets of Franklin, there is something for everyone. This mix of low cost of living and ease of living in Tennessee brings up an important question: what specific resources and amenities make Tennessee not only a good financial choice for retirement, but also a great place to live?

Key Things to Think About

For retirees, getting good health care is one of the most important things, and Tennessee has made a lot of progress in this important area. Nashville, Memphis, Knoxville, and Chattanooga are the state's four largest cities. Each has world-class medical facilities that are on par with those in much larger cities. Vanderbilt University Medical Center in Nashville, for instance, consistently ranks among the nation's top hospitals, offering cutting-edge treatments and specialized senior care programs. But what really makes Tennessee stand out is its dedication to making health care more accessible outside of cities.

Tennessee has put a lot of money into rural health programs because they know that many retirees like the peace and low cost of living in rural areas. More and more modern medical clinics, telemedicine programs, and mobile health units are coming to small towns and rural areas. You don't have to choose between living in a quiet small town and being able to get good medical care; Tennessee lets you have both. With the state's network of regional hospitals and specialty clinics, you'll never have to travel far to get full medical protection.

In addition to good healthcare, Tennessee's cultural landscape gives retirees a rich life that belies its low cost of living. The state's musical history isn't just something to see as a tourist; it's a real part of everyday life. In Nashville, you might start your day at a café where a new singer-songwriter plays music while you eat breakfast. You could spend your evening in Memphis taking a walk down Beale Street, where the blues come from old clubs that have been hosting legends for generations. Music festivals, concert series, and jam sessions happen all the time in the state, even in smaller towns. These events keep the artistic spirit alive.

This lively cultural life goes beyond music. From Civil War battlefields to civil rights landmarks, Tennessee's historical sites tell the story of America as a whole. The state has four distinct seasons, which make it fun to do things all year long, from hiking to see wildflowers in the Great Smoky Mountains in the spring to art festivals in cute town squares in the fall. Tennessee's community calendar stays busy all year, unlike some retirement spots where things slow down during certain times of the year.

When you look at the little things in life, the financial benefits of living in Tennessee become even clearer.

The state's housing markets are a great deal, with well-kept homes in desirable neighborhoods often going for prices that would barely cover a down payment in many coastal states. Maintenance costs, like lawn care and home repairs, are also affordable because of competitive labor markets and fair service rates. Home, auto, and health insurance rates in Tennessee tend to be lower than national averages. This makes retirement in Tennessee more financially stable overall.

The most important thing about all of these benefits is that they work together to make communities where retirees can really thrive. There are active senior centers, lifelong learning programs through local colleges, and a huge number of volunteer opportunities in the cities and towns of Tennessee. The famous "volunteer spirit" of the state is more than just a slogan; it shows up in close-knit neighborhoods where people look out for each other and welcome newcomers with true Southern hospitality.

Tennessee gives middle-class retirees a chance to live well without constantly worrying about money, which is becoming more and more rare in today's world. You can reach your retirement goals no matter if you like the liveliness of cities, the peace and quiet of mountain towns, or the beauty of small towns in the country. With its strong healthcare system, wide range of cultural activities, and low cost of living, Tennessee is not only a place to retire, but also a place to really enjoy your golden years.

The best thing about Tennessee as a place to retire is that it can surprise you. While Florida and Arizona may dominate retirement conversations, those who choose Tennessee often find themselves wondering why they didn't consider it sooner. The state has beautiful natural scenery that changes with the seasons, from misty mornings in the Great Smoky Mountains to sunsets over the Mississippi River. You can get ideas for your next adventure any time of the year.

Consider the story of Mark and Laura Grant, who initially planned to retire to Florida but stopped in Tennessee during their research trip. "We were just passing through," Laura says, "but after spending a week exploring different towns and talking to locals, we realized we'd found something special." After living in Franklin for three years, they've become unofficial ambassadors for the city. They say it has the perfect mix of cultural amenities, outdoor activities, and what they call "front-porch friendliness."

What makes Tennessee particularly appealing for middle-class retirees is the freedom that comes with financial stability. When the cost of living goes down and the quality of life goes up, you can try new hobbies, travel more, or just spend more time with family without having to worry about money all the time. Whether it's taking art classes in Gatlinburg, joining a golf league in Crossville (known as the "Golf Capital of Tennessee"), or finally learning to play guitar in Nashville, retirees find their dollars stretch further while their opportunities expand.

The state's central location makes it even more appealing. Because Tennessee is in the middle of the South and the Midwest, it's easy to get to see family and friends. Major airports in Nashville, Memphis, and Knoxville make it easy to get to faraway places, and the state's extensive interstate system makes it easy to get away for the weekend. In one day, you can wake up in the mountains, eat lunch in Music City, and watch the sun go down over the river.

Tennesse's dedication to growth while keeping costs low points the way to a bright future for retirees. The state continues to attract major employers, leading to improved infrastructure and amenities without the dramatic cost increases seen in other popular retirement destinations. In order to meet the needs of an active retirement population, new healthcare facilities are being built, cultural attractions are growing, and community programs are always changing.

For those considering retirement in Tennessee, the best advice might be to come for a visit – but pack lightly. A lot of retired people have found that what starts out as an exploratory trip ends up with them calling a real estate agent in the area. Tennessee is a great place to retire because it has great natural beauty, cultural diversity, financial benefits, and easy access to health care. If you're interested in the lively cities, the peaceful mountains, or the charming small towns of Tennessee, retirement there will feel less like slowing down and more like starting a new and exciting part of your life.

Before you decide where to retire, you might want to take a closer look at Tennessee. Visit during different seasons, explore various communities, and talk to local retirees. You might find, like many others have, that the Volunteer State is the best place to retire because it is both affordable and nice to live. Tennessee isn't just a place to retire; it's a place to do well.

3

Michigan and the Great Lakes: Why They Are Important

Most people think of sandy beaches and palm trees when they think of retirement. More and more smart retirees are finding out what Michiganders have always known: the Great Lakes State is a beautiful alternative that is also easy on the wallet. Michigan's natural splendor, combined with its surprisingly retirement-friendly financial landscape, creates an opportunity for middle-class retirees to live a lifestyle that would be financially out of reach in many traditional retirement havens.

The natural beauty of Michigan is not only stunning but also easy to get to. Imagine drinking your coffee in the morning on a deck with a view of one of the Great Lakes. The waves of the freshwater lake would hit the sandy shores, making them look just as good as any ocean beach. In coastal states, waterfront property sells for crazy high prices, but in Michigan, lakefront living is actually possible at a reasonable price. From the dramatic dunes of Lake Michigan to the rugged shores of Lake Superior, the state boasts more coastline than any state except Alaska, yet at a fraction of the cost you'd find in oceanfront communities.

There are many financial benefits to retiring in Michigan besides just finding cheap waterfront property. The state has done a lot to become more tax-friendly for retirees by putting in place policies that help them get more out of their money. Michigan is one of the friendliest states when it comes to retirement income. Pension income and other retirement distributions can be deducted in large amounts. People who get Social Security benefits don't have to pay any state taxes on them, and people aged 67 and up can get extra tax breaks that can make their overall tax burden much lower.

What makes Michigan unique is that it offers a high-quality way of life at prices that are more typical of the Midwest. Friends who live in coastal states may have to downsize in order to afford retirement, but retirees in Michigan often find that they can keep or even improve their current lifestyle. Many nice neighborhoods in Michigan have housing costs that are 30–50% less than similar coastal areas. This means that you can spend more of your money on enjoying life instead of just keeping it up. This cost advantage goes beyond housing and includes things like groceries and entertainment. It's a complete value proposition that smart retirees are becoming more and more interested in.

But Michigan's appeal isn't just about saving money; it's also about opening up new possibilities. The state's big seasonal changes don't make retirement less possible; they make it more possible. As we talk about the unique benefits of living in Michigan, you'll see that each season brings new chances for fun, community, and personal growth. This means that retirement here is anything but retirement. The question isn't whether you can afford to retire in Michigan – it's whether you can afford not to consider it.

Key Things to Think About

Every season brings a new look to Michigan's landscape, making life there like a work of art that is always being painted. Michigan isn't just about snow in the winter or beaches in the summer. Many retirees find that the state has just the right amount of activities and opportunities all year long. This natural cycle keeps life fresh and interesting, preventing the monotony that some retirees experience in unchanging climates.

Michigan summers are nothing less than magical. In the south, retirees tend to stay inside during the hot summer months, but people in Michigan love all the things they can do outside.

```
Imagine taking care of a garden in the morning while the weather
is perfect, sailing on clear lakes in the afternoon, and going to
free concerts in parks by lakes in the evening.
```

The state's thousands of inland lakes and streams offer a wide range of activities, from peaceful kayaking to great fishing, without the crowds and high costs that come with coastal recreation areas.

Michigan turns into a painting of bright colors as summer ends and fall begins. The state's vast forests put on a show that draws visitors from around the world, but as a resident, you'll have front-row seats to this spectacular display right in your own neighborhood. Fall color tours turn into unplanned adventures, and some people plan whole vacations around the views they see on their way to the store. Local farmers' markets overflow with fresh apples, pumpkins, and harvest bounty, while communities celebrate the season with festivals that highlight Michigan's rich agricultural heritage.

Winter in Michigan is far more than the snowy stereotype outsiders might imagine. Active retirees are in for a lot of great opportunities this time of year. You can get low-impact, high-reward exercise right outside your door by cross-country skiing and snowshoeing. You don't even need to pay a lot of money for a ski resort membership. Many retirees discover a new passion for winter photography, bird watching, or simply enjoying the peaceful beauty of snow-covered landscapes from the comfort of their cozy homes. There are lots of indoor activities in community centers and libraries, like art classes and book clubs, so people can stay in touch all year.

When you look at the specifics, the economic benefits of living in Michigan become even clearer. Even though the state's property taxes aren't the lowest in the country, they are balanced out by the state's higher overall cost of living and large retirement income tax breaks. There are a lot of lakefront communities with home prices that look like typos in coastal real estate listings. Most of the time, a nice three-bedroom house with views of or access to water costs less than a one-bedroom condo in Florida or California.

The strong sense of community in Michigan adds another level of value that is harder to measure but can't be ignored. The many college towns in the state, such as Ann Arbor, East Lansing, and Marquette, offer a wide range of cultural events and chances to keep learning throughout life. These college towns have a friendly, small-town feel while still offering access to high-quality healthcare, a wide range of dining options, and endless entertainment options.

When it comes to health care, Michigan has some of the best institutions in the world, such as the University of Michigan Medical Center and Beaumont Health System. The state has a large network of regional healthcare centers that make sure everyone can get good medical care, even in smaller towns. Many retirees find it comforting to know that they can get top-notch medical care without having to travel to big cities or pay the high prices that come with it.

The state's commitment to senior-friendly communities is evident in its growing network of walking trails, senior centers, and recreational programs specifically designed for active adults. Many communities in Michigan have embraced the idea of "aging in place" by creating neighborhoods and services that help seniors stay active and independent while still being connected to their neighborhood. Michigan retirees can stay involved in their communities and make a difference in a lot of different ways, from volunteering at nature centers to mentoring programs in schools.

Most importantly, Michigan gives retirees the space and freedom to really enjoy their retirement, which is becoming less common in today's world. Because the cost of living is lower in Michigan, you can afford the space you need to start a small garden, have family get-togethers, or do hobbies that need a bit more space. The state has a lot of different landscapes that make it perfect for any kind of retirement you can imagine, from quiet life by a lake to busy city life.

The combination of natural beauty, affordability, and strong communities creates a retirement experience that many find surprisingly complete. While some might worry about adapting to Michigan's seasons, most retirees discover that the changing weather adds richness to their lives, creating distinct chapters in each year's story. A place where you can build the retirement you've always wanted without lowering your standard of living or risking your money.

```
When people retire in Michigan, their stories often start with
doubt and end with discovery.
```

Take the Wang family, who moved to Grand Haven three years ago from California. "Friends thought we were crazy to leave the Pacific for the Great Lakes," Susie says. "Now, every summer and fall, they come to visit. They are amazed that our lakefront home cost less than their one-bedroom condo." But what's more, they can see how full our lives have become.

Michigan's best-kept secret is what the Wang family and many others have found: it's not just a place to retire, it's a place to reinvent retirement. Here, middle-class retirees find themselves with the financial freedom and physical space to pursue dreams that might have seemed out of reach elsewhere. The opportunities grow as you broaden your horizons. You could finally write that novel in a cozy lake house, start a small vineyard in Michigan's rich soil, or just have enough extra rooms for when your kids and grandchildren come to visit.

Another strong benefit is that the state is in a strategic location. Michigan, which is in the middle of the Great Lakes region, is close to Chicago, Toronto, and other big cities but also offers a peaceful escape from the noise and chaos of the cities. Detroit and Grand Rapids both have international airports that connect to the rest of the world. Driving along the Great Lakes is a beautiful way to see charming coastal towns and hidden gems that even people who have lived there their whole lives are still finding.

Looking ahead, Michigan's commitment to developing its communities while preserving their character suggests a bright future for retirees. Along with the restoration of historic districts, new cultural venues are opening. Healthcare networks keep getting bigger and better at what they do. Every year, more and more bike and walking paths and trails are built, linking communities and giving people new ways to explore. One of the best things about this market is that property values are going up steadily over time. This protects your investment without the wild speculation that has kept so many retirees out of other markets.

If you're interested in what Michigan has to offer, try going during more than one season. Come in the summer, when beach towns are busy and music festivals fill the air. Come back in the fall, when the leaves are changing color and the farm markets are full of food that was grown that year. Enjoy a peaceful winter morning when new snow covers the ground and turns it into a beautiful, pristine world. Watch spring unfold as trillium carpets the forest floor and cherry blossoms paint the air pink.

Talk to retired people in the area; you can find them walking around downtown, taking care of community gardens, or hanging out at cafes by the lake. Their stories often share a common thread: they came to Michigan for the value but stayed for the quality of life. A lot of people found that what looked like a compromise on paper turned out to be an improvement.

Michigan retirement isn't for everyone – and that's part of its charm. For people who see each season as a chance to do something new. It's for people who prefer real communities to ones with gates. People who know that real luxury isn't about how much money you have, but about being able to live your life however you want.

Remember, people retire to Florida every year without a second thought, but choosing Michigan reflects a deeper wisdom. In retirement, you shouldn't try to fit in with everyone else. Instead, you should find a place where you can write your own story. More and more middle-class retirees are finding their home in the Great Lakes State, where the water is clean and the people are friendly.

4

Arizona: Living in the Desert with Modern Conveniences

Most people who think about retiring in Arizona picture expensive golf communities in Scottsdale or large suburbs of Phoenix. For smart middle-class retirees, though, there's a better way to live in the desert—one that doesn't require a CEO's pension or lower quality of life. As with anything else, the key is to know where to look and how Arizona's unique benefits can help you.

Imagine waking up to a beautiful desert sunrise in a cozy home in a charming town like Casa Grande, Prescott Valley, or Sierra Vista instead of a pricey mansion in Scottsdale. These new retirement communities have the same beautiful desert views and modern conveniences as their more well-known neighbors, but they are more affordable for middle-class families. You'll find well-thought-out neighborhoods in these communities where desert style meets everyday life, and where your retirement dollars will go a lot further.

A lot of people who want to retire don't know that Arizona's climate isn't just endless sunshine; it's actually good for your health and can have a big effect on your quality of life. The low humidity and clean, dry air in the state make it a natural therapy for people with breathing problems or arthritis. Long-term residents often say that moving to the desert made them less dependent on certain medications and helped them move around better. Being comfortable all year isn't the only reason to have sunshine; it's also a way to stay active and healthy all year long.

Arizona is at the forefront of building smart infrastructure, which may be its most underrated strength. Other places to retire have systems that are getting old, but Arizona's newer communities are made with the future in mind. Many homes have solar panels on their roofs, which can help seniors on fixed incomes save a lot of money on their energy bills. Modern medical facilities aren't just spread out in big cities; they're strategically placed all over the state to make sure that people can always get good care.

But what really makes modern life in Arizona unique is how it's changing what it means to be sophisticated in the desert. People used to have to choose between golf courses and cactus gardens when they retired here. At a surprisingly low cost of living, Arizona today offers a wide range of activities that combine the beauty of nature with the ease of city life. This change brings up an interesting question: How can middle-class retirees enjoy all that Arizona has to offer without spending too much? The answer lies in understanding how the state's unique mix of health, lifestyle, and economic benefits works.

Key Things to Think About

The real magic of retiring in Arizona is found in the little things that you do every day. Take the price of energy as an example. Friends who live in other states fear their summer cooling bills, but retirees in Arizona are often pleasantly surprised. It's not just an environmental statement that the state is supporting solar power; it's also a practical solution that can cut monthly costs by a large amount. A lot of retirement communities are made to be energy-efficient. For example, homes in desert-smart communities stay cooler on their own and utility bills are lower.

Arizona's healthcare has changed a lot over the years because it has been serving retirement communities for so long. Not only is the state's medical infrastructure impressive for how well it works, but it's also easy for people to get to. Big healthcare systems have set up networks of clinics and specialty centers all over the state because they know that retirees would rather get great care without having to drive into big cities. Smaller, easier-to-navigate towns like Green Valley and Payson offer high-tech medical care where doctors still take the time to know each patient by name.

The way the state encourages active adult living has also grown up. These days, retirement communities in Arizona aren't separate areas; they're well-planned neighborhoods that balance privacy with community. Instead of living in a gated community, many retirees choose to live in active neighborhoods with people of all ages. These neighborhoods have all the amenities retirees want and also have lots of interactions between generations that keep life interesting. At nearby community centers, you can find everything from pottery classes to pickleball tournaments. Hiking trails give you quick access to Arizona's beautiful natural scenery.

Many people who move to Arizona are surprised by how culturally rich the state is, especially in its smaller cities and towns. People know about Sedona's art galleries, but towns like Tubac and Bisbee also have lively art scenes at prices that most people can afford. Theaters, museums, and music venues in the area offer year-round fun without the costs or hassles of big cities. The food scene has grown so big that it's no longer just Southwest food. New restaurants and farmers markets all over the state serve fresh, varied food.

Some new retirement spots have become very valuable for middle-class retirees thanks to smart growth initiatives. Cities like Maricopa and San Tan Valley have new roads and other amenities, but housing costs are still much lower than the national average. Living in the desert doesn't have to cost a lot of money; you just need to plan ahead and be willing to look beyond the obvious options.

While private golf clubs get all the attention, the state's real wealth is in its public spaces. There are miles of hiking and biking trails, well-kept state parks, and a lot of places to watch birds or take pictures all year long that don't charge membership fees. Many retirees find that their favorite things to do are the ones that don't cost anything, like taking early morning walks in the desert or watching the sunset from their back patio.

Technology is becoming more and more important in Arizona retirement living. In the state's newer towns, high-speed internet is built in as a standard feature, not an extra. This infrastructure helps with a lot of things, like telemedicine appointments and staying in touch with family across the country. Many retirement communities in Arizona use smart home technologies to help them control their energy use, keep their homes safe, and make daily life easier.

You can choose your level of luxury in Arizona, which makes it a great place for middle-class retirees. Communities like Prescott and Sierra Vista show that comfort and quality don't have to cost a lot of money. Scottsdale and Paradise Valley are examples of the high end of desert living. In these places, retirees can enjoy resort-style amenities, busy social calendars, and high-quality medical care without having to worry about money.

The economic foundations that support retirement in Arizona keep getting stronger. The state's growing tech industry makes services better and keeps local economies stable. Property values have been going up steadily and steadily, which is good for retirees who see their homes as both safe places to live and investments. Tourism remains strong, supporting a robust infrastructure of restaurants, entertainment venues, and cultural attractions that residents enjoy year-round.

```
The real beauty of retiring in Arizona isn't in the high-end
resorts or private golf communities; it's in the little things
that make life in the desert so special.
```

Just ask Peter and Hannah Rodriguez, who moved from Chicago to Prescott three years ago. "At first, we were worried about giving up seasons for sunshine," Hannah says. "Now we tell time by the color of the desert wildflowers, the sound of the monsoons, and the most beautiful sunsets we've ever seen." Our friends back home think we've moved to a resort, but we're just getting by on our teacher's pension.

What the Rodriguez family and others have found is Arizona's best-kept secret: there is a sweet spot where middle-class retirees can thrive that is halfway between basic retirement living and high-end developments. In the morning, you might go for a hike through desert trails that are full of flowers, and then you might get a cappuccino at a local café where the barista knows your name. Where "running errands" means driving past red rock formations or hills covered with saguaros that still take your breath away after living here for years.

The math behind retirement in Arizona often surprises people who are new to the state in a good way. With solar panels, lots of sunshine means lower utility bills. Living outside all year naturally lowers entertainment costs; who needs pricey hobbies when nature gives us a show every day? Because of the healthy climate and active lifestyle that seems to come naturally here, many retirees also see a drop in their health care costs.

If you're interested in what Arizona has to offer, try going there during different seasons, not just the obvious ones. Come during the monsoon season, when huge storms paint the desert in colors that seem impossible to achieve. Experience a winter morning when frost delicately edges desert plants, then melts away to reveal a perfect 70-degree day. In the spring, when the wildflowers bloom, the seemingly harsh landscape looks like a painter's palette.

Don't just look at the usual places to retire. Spend time in places like Casa Grande, where creative revitalizations are happening in old downtown areas. Visit the towns in the Verde Valley. These towns are becoming wine regions, and farm-to-table isn't just a trend; it's a way of life. Visit the lakeside trails in Prescott or the bird sanctuaries in Sierra Vista. Most of the time, these alternatives to well-known spots offer the same amenities for a lot less money.

The future of retirement in Arizona looks especially good for people from the middle class. As technology hubs grow beyond Phoenix, they bring better services and amenities to the towns that are close by. Solar initiatives continue to make desert living more sustainable and affordable. As healthcare networks grow, they bring world-class medical care to more places in the state.

Some people might not be able to retire in Arizona, which is part of its appeal. It's for people who find beauty in subtle changes, who appreciate the drama of a monsoon storm rolling across the desert. People who know that luxury isn't about spending a lot of money but about being able to live each day your own way.

Remember that if you want to retire in Arizona, you don't have to go to the most expensive communities like everyone else. It's about being smart enough to look in places no one else has, to find those sweet spots where middle-class dreams and desert realities meet. It's about learning that you don't need a lot of money to live a good life—you just need to know where to look.

Arizona has a lot to offer, whether you're looking for a healthy climate, a way of life full of outdoor activities, or just the freedom to retire without worrying about money. Beyond the famous destinations and luxury developments lies another Arizona – one where middle-class retirees aren't just surviving, but thriving.

It's interesting how the desert can show you what's really important in life. Perhaps that's why so many find not just a retirement destination here, but a place where they finally feel at home.

5

Delaware: The Eastern Option That Is Good for Taxes

When people from the East Coast think of their golden years, they often picture the beaches in Florida or the mild weather in the Carolinas. In the meantime, one of the best places in America to retire financially is nestled between them, offering benefits that smart middle-class retirees find harder and harder to resist. Delaware, the "Small Wonder," has emerged as a strategic choice for those who want to maintain their Eastern connections while maximizing their retirement dollars.

Let's start with what catches most retirees' attention: Delaware's remarkable tax advantages. In a region where high taxes make retirees want to move west or south, Delaware is a tax-friendly haven. Imagine going into a store and paying the exact price that's written on the tag. You wouldn't have to figure out sales tax. We're not just talking about saving a few dollars on purchases; this is about keeping more of your retirement income where it belongs: in your pocket.

The story of Delaware's property taxes is just as interesting. People who live in New Jersey, New York, and Maryland see their property taxes go up every year, but people who live in Delaware have some of the lowest property tax rates in the country. This isn't just about savings for middle-class retirees; it's also about being able to plan ahead. When you can accurately forecast your housing costs years into the future, retirement planning becomes less about survival and more about enjoyment.

But Delaware's appeal goes far beyond its tax advantages. The state is in a great spot because it is in the middle of everything the East Coast has to offer. Imagine having family gatherings where people from Boston to Richmond can come without having to book flights. Picture taking short day trips to the museums in Philadelphia, the harbor in Baltimore, or the cultural sites in Washington, D.C. Delaware is a beautiful option for retirees who still want to be close to big cities but don't want to pay the high costs of living in a big city.

The real thing that makes Delaware stand out, though, is how it combines these useful benefits with a surprisingly rich coastal lifestyle. While Florida's beaches get all the attention, Delaware's coastline has its own unique maritime charm, and it has a lot fewer people and much lower insurance rates. With all of these financial and lifestyle benefits, Delaware has to offer, it begs the question of how middle-class retirees can best take advantage of it all.

Major Things to Think About

Life in Delaware unfolds with a particular charm that combines coastal living with practical advantages. Take the beach towns as an example. Many people visit Rehoboth Beach and Lewes during the summer, but all year long, the towns feel more like a close-knit neighborhood than a vacation spot. Retirees come here to find that they can walk along the Atlantic in the morning without having to pay the high prices of Atlantic City or Hampton Beach.

The state's approach to coastal living deserves special attention. While Florida's coastline is prone to hurricanes and New England's winters are harsh, Delaware's beaches offer a more moderate sea experience. This advantage is reflected in the cost of insurance: coastal property insurance in Delaware often costs a lot less than in other Eastern seaboard states. This means that for middle-class retirees, living on the beach isn't just a dream; it's a real possibility.

Delaware's sea activities go beyond just relaxing on the beach. With all the inland bays and waterways, you can go boating, fishing, and doing water sports for a lot less money than at marinas on the ocean. By kayaking or bird watching along the wetlands, retired couples often find hobbies that don't cost much but give them a lot of enjoyment. The state's many nature preserves and wildlife refuges offer fun activities all year long for photographers, nature lovers, and anyone else who enjoys the beauty of nature.

The financial benefits of Delaware living become even more apparent when you examine day-to-day life. Delaware has big tax breaks for retirees, on top of not having a sales tax. People who are 60 or older and get Social Security benefits are not taxed, and the state gives them large pension exclusions. Just what does this mean in real life? It means that many retirees can eat out more often, try new hobbies, or travel without having to constantly watch their pennies.

Delaware's commitment to the health and happiness of retirees is shown in its healthcare system. There are large medical centers in Wilmington, Dover, and the beach areas that offer great care without being too big like hospitals in big cities. Specialized medical care is never more than a short drive away because the state is not very big. This is an important factor for retirees to consider. A lot of people find that the combination of good healthcare and lower costs of living lets them get better insurance than they could in nearby states.

The small size of the state is often seen as a problem, but it actually works out well for retirees. Everything seems manageable, from community groups to government services.

Want to get a new driver's license? Lines are likely to be shorter and service will be more personal than in bigger states. Want to get involved in things going on in your community? Having connections in a small town can help you find your niche and make a difference.

For newcomers, Delaware's arts and entertainment scenes are a pleasant surprise. The state is close to big cities, so you can see world-class shows and museums without having to pay the high costs of living in a city. Local arts scenes, especially along the river in Wilmington and in beach towns, offer regular entertainment without the hassles of traffic or parking. Many retirees start going to local theaters and music venues on a regular basis, enjoying cultural activities that would cost a lot in bigger cities.

Delaware's weather is worth mentioning because it's a good compromise for retirees on the East Coast. You'll see all four seasons, but none of them will be as bad as the winters in New England or the summers in Florida. Spring and fall last longer here, so there are longer periods of great weather for doing things outside. It's still mild enough outside to do regular exercise even in the winter, which is an important part of staying active in retirement.

Because the state cares about education and lifelong learning, retirees can find new opportunities they didn't expect. Osher Lifelong Learning Institute (OLLI) programs at the University of Delaware provide intellectual stimulation and social connections without putting too much pressure on students to do well in school. Many retired people take classes in everything from digital photography to local history. These classes help them keep their minds sharp and help them meet new people.

The best thing about Delaware for retirees is that they can live
comfortably without worrying about money all the time. This is
becoming less common on the East Coast.

The combination of tax advantages, reasonable housing costs, and strategic location creates a retirement experience that feels more expansive than restrictive. Whether you want to live near the coast, experience culture, or just stay close to family on the East Coast, Delaware is a great place for middle-class retirees to thrive instead of just surviving.

The best way to see how hidden gem-like Delaware retirement can be is to hear from people who have already found it. Take Carole and James Murphy as an example. They were going to retire in Florida but stopped in Delaware to see friends. "We came for the weekend and stayed for a week," Carole says. "By the end of that week, we were calling apartment renters." We learned that we could get everything we wanted—access to the beach, cultural activities, and being close to family—without spending all of our savings. We're still pinching ourselves after five years.

The Murphy family and others have found that Delaware has something that is becoming harder to find on the East Coast: financial breathing room along with location benefits that keep life interesting. While their friends in neighboring states worry about rising property taxes and living costs, retirees in Delaware often have extra money to spend on hobbies, travel, or just enjoying the little things in life without feeling bad about it.

The strategic value of Delaware's location continues to appreciate as travel costs rise elsewhere. Think about the math behind family ties: when kids and grandkids can drive to visit instead of flying, families get together more often. Many retirees find that they host more often and become the natural place for family gatherings. Shopping in Delaware is tax-free and prices are reasonable, which makes this role easier.

Looking ahead, Delaware's future looks especially good for people who are retired. While keeping its tax-friendly stance, the state continues to put money into coastal infrastructure. As new towns are being built, they often include walking paths, community centers, and easy access to medical facilities to meet the needs of retirees. As telehealth services and specialty medical care grow, Delaware becomes a more appealing place for people who care about getting access to health care.

Check out Delaware at different times of the year and don't just be a tourist if you're interested in what it has to offer. Spend time in local coffee shops, strike up conversations at farmers' markets, attend a community event. You'll probably notice something different: a lively but not overbearing pace of life, lots of things to do without getting worn out, and a sense of community that you don't always find in bigger states.

Don't just go to the obvious places. Rehoboth Beach and Lewes are both beautiful coastal towns that draw people in, but Milton, Georgetown, and Dover also have their own unique benefits. There are a lot of different places to live in Delaware, from quiet historic districts to busy cultural hubs, so retirees can find the perfect place for them.

```
One of the things that makes Delaware a great place to retire is
that it's not for everyone. It's for people who understand that
bigger isn't always better, who appreciate the value of strategic
location, and who recognize that true luxury isn't about prestige
addresses but about having the freedom to enjoy life on your own
terms.
```

Remember that picking Delaware as a place to retire isn't just following the crowd; it's seeing a chance that other people might miss. Some retirees automatically move to states that are known for being good places to retire, but smart middle-class retirees are finding that this small state has a lot to offer. From tax benefits that keep more money in your pocket to a location that keeps you connected to everything you love about the East Coast, Delaware proves that sometimes the best retirement choices come in small packages.

In strange ways, the "Small Wonder" state lives up to its name. It gives you joy in the little things, like sunrise walks on beaches that aren't crowded, unplanned visits from family who can easily get to you, shopping without having to figure out sales tax, and the peace of mind that comes from knowing your retirement dollars will go further here.

For those seeking an East Coast retirement that combines fiscal responsibility with quality of life, Delaware deserves more than a passing glance. You should really think about it as a place where your retirement dreams could come true and grow, while still letting you stay in touch with family, friends, and the area you love.

6

South Carolina: Southern Charm Meets Affordability

Few states capture the essence of gracious retirement living quite like South Carolina. For middle-class retirees seeking the perfect blend of affordability and quality of life, the Palmetto State stands out as an increasingly popular choice.

When you think of retirement in South Carolina, you might picture yourself sipping sweet tea on a wraparound porch or teeing off on a world-class golf course. While these iconic images certainly ring true, the Palmetto State offers middle-class retirees far more than just Southern stereotypes – it provides a compelling combination of financial benefits, lifestyle opportunities, and natural beauty that makes it one of America's most attractive retirement destinations.

Why South Carolina Catches Retirees' Eyes

What draws middle-class retirees to South Carolina isn't just the famous Southern hospitality – it's the state's remarkable ability to stretch retirement dollars while delivering an enviable quality of life. The cost of living runs approximately 10-15% below the national average, with housing costs being particularly favorable. In many South Carolina communities, retirees can find quality homes for significantly less than what they'd pay in Northern or Western states.

The climate deserves special mention. South Carolina offers what many consider the "sweet spot" of weather patterns – mild winters that rarely see snow, extended springs and falls perfect for outdoor activities, and summers that, while warm, provide the perfect excuse to head to the beach or mountains. This climate allows for year-round outdoor activities, reducing the need for the seasonal lifestyle adjustments required in more northern states.

Tax Benefits That Make Sense for Retirees

South Carolina rolls out the welcome mat for retirees with several tax advantages that can make a real difference in retirement planning:

- Social Security benefits are completely tax-exempt at the state level
- Retirees can deduct up to $10,000 of qualified retirement income from their state taxes
- Seniors 65 and older can claim an additional $15,000 deduction on their state income taxes
- Property taxes tend to be lower than the national average, with additional homestead exemptions available for seniors

Geographic Diversity: Choose Your Perfect Setting

One of South Carolina's most appealing aspects is its geographic variety. The state naturally divides into three distinct regions, each offering its own lifestyle advantages:

The Coast (The Lowcountry)

- Historic Charleston with its award-winning restaurants and cultural scene
- Myrtle Beach's 60-mile "Grand Strand" offering affordable coastal living
- The peaceful Sea Islands, including Hilton Head, for those seeking upscale resort living
- Smaller coastal communities like Beaufort and Georgetown that provide charm without the tourist crowds

The Midlands

- Columbia, the state capital, with its university town energy and cultural offerings
- Smaller cities like Aiken and Camden that offer horse country living
- Lake Murray and Lake Marion for waterfront living at reasonable prices
- Strong medical infrastructure centered around major hospitals

The Upstate

- Greenville's revitalized downtown and growing cultural scene
- Beautiful mountain views and cooler temperatures
- Proximity to the Blue Ridge Mountains for outdoor enthusiasts
- Strong manufacturing economy providing part-time work opportunities

> When it comes to financial benefits, South Carolina makes retirement dollars stretch further through thoughtful tax policies and housing market advantages.

Beyond the impressive tax benefits already mentioned, seniors find particular comfort in the state's approach to property taxes. The homestead exemption provides significant relief for primary residences, and many counties offer additional age-based exemptions that can substantially reduce annual property tax bills.

The housing market remains remarkably approachable for middle-class retirees. Whether you're looking for a cozy downtown condo in Greenville or a spacious single-family home in Columbia, you'll find prices that compare favorably to other popular retirement destinations. Even in desirable coastal areas, careful shoppers can still find reasonable options, particularly if they're willing to look a few miles inland from the beach.

Insurance costs in South Carolina tend to be manageable for most retirees, though location plays a key role. While coastal properties may require additional hurricane coverage, inland homes typically enjoy very reasonable insurance rates. Health insurance options are plentiful, especially in and around major metropolitan areas, and auto insurance rates generally run below the national average.

The lifestyle advantages of retiring in South Carolina extend far beyond the financial benefits. Golf enthusiasts find themselves in paradise, with hundreds of courses scattered throughout the state. From municipal courses that offer affordable play to world-renowned destinations like those in Hilton Head, there's something for every skill level and budget. Many communities are

Cultural attractions abound throughout the state, offering enriching experiences for retirees with varied interests. Charleston's Spoleto Festival USA brings world-class performing arts to the region each spring. Columbia's Riverbanks Zoo and Botanical Garden provides year-round entertainment and educational opportunities. The Peace Center in Greenville hosts Broadway tours and symphony performances, while smaller venues across the state offer intimate cultural experiences in historic settings.

The state's rich history comes alive through its many preserved sites and museums. From Revolutionary War battlefields to antebellum homes, history buffs find endless opportunities to explore and learn. Many retirees discover a second calling as volunteer docents at these sites, sharing South Carolina's heritage with visitors from around the world.

Active living takes many forms in South Carolina. Besides golf, retirees enjoy tennis, pickleball, and water sports. The state's extensive park system offers hiking trails for all ability levels, while coastal areas provide opportunities for fishing, boating, and beachcombing. Community centers throughout the state host fitness classes and social activities specifically designed for seniors.

Perhaps most importantly, South Carolina offers a sense of community that many retirees find lacking in other destinations. Whether you choose a planned active-adult community or a traditional neighborhood, you'll find locals and fellow transplants alike ready to welcome you into their social circles. Church groups, civic organizations, and hobby clubs provide natural ways to meet people and build meaningful connections.

The combination of geographic diversity, financial benefits, and lifestyle advantages makes South Carolina a compelling choice for middle-class retirees. While the state's charm and hospitality might first catch your eye, it's the practical benefits and everyday livability that make it a place you'll want to call home. Whether you choose the coastal lowlands, the midland's historic towns, or the mountain-view upstate, South Carolina offers middle-class retirees the opportunity to create the retirement lifestyle they've always dreamed about without compromising their financial security.

> South Carolina's charm as a retirement destination lies not just in its famous beaches or golf courses, but in its remarkable ability to offer multiple versions of the good life at middle-class prices.

Take Elizabeth and Jim Connor, who moved from Maryland to Greenville three years ago. "Everyone expected us to choose Myrtle Beach or Hilton Head," Elizabeth says. "Instead, we found this lively city tucked between the Blue Ridge Mountains." We have four real seasons, a great downtown area, and our savings for retirement go so much further here. We can still go to the beach whenever we want, but we don't have to pay the high summer prices.

The Connors and others have found South Carolina's secret advantage: its varied landscape makes it possible to live almost any kind of retirement lifestyle you can think of. Each area has its own mix of amenities and prices, from the historic charm of the Midlands to the coastal towns of the Lowcountry and the mountain towns of the Upstate. You don't have to choose between a good quality of life and financial security. You can have both in places like Clemson, Aiken, and Beaufort.

Looking ahead, South Carolina's future looks especially good for middle-class retirees. The state continues to bring in big businesses, especially in the Upstate area. This has led to better infrastructure and healthcare options all over the state. In order to meet the needs of active retirees, new cultural venues are opening, walking trails are getting longer, and community programs are changing. One of the best things about this market is that property values are going up steadily over time. This protects your investment without the wild speculation that has kept so many retirees out of other markets.

People who are interested in what South Carolina has to offer might want to try this: go beyond the tourist spots. The downtown area of Greenville has won a lot of awards. Come to Clemson on a weekend when there are no games to enjoy its small-town feel. Visit the horse country near Aiken or the historic waterfront in Georgetown. Each area has its own style of Southern living, and the prices are often surprisingly low.

Finding the most famous place to retire in South Carolina isn't the key to middle-class success; it's finding the face of the state that fits your retirement dreams the best. South Carolina has places to live that fit your needs and your budget, whether you want to live in a busy downtown area, a quiet mountain retreat, or a coastal town where everyone knows your name.

Remember that picking South Carolina as a place to retire isn't just about going to the most expensive towns. It means being smart enough to know that your quality of life, not your zip code or club memberships, is what defines true luxury in retirement. Its lowlands are full of sweetgrass baskets, and its upstate has rolling hills. South Carolina shows that you can still have Southern charm on a middle-class budget.

In the end, retirement in South Carolina gives you choices, which is becoming more and more rare these days. You won't have to choose between your retirement dreams and your financial security if you want to live in the country or near the ocean, with views of the mountains or the breeze from the ocean. If you know you can retire in a place that feels like it's been waiting for you all along, that might be the real promise of Southern comfort.

7

New Mexico: Southwest's Secret Gem

Most people who are thinking about retiring in the Southwest talk about Arizona and Nevada. But smart middle-class retirees are finding New Mexico's charming secret: you can live in beautiful scenery and learn about rich cultural traditions without spending a lot of money. The Land of Enchantment offers something that is becoming harder to find in retirement communities today: a real experience at a reasonable price.

When you see the Sandia Mountains, you'll know why they're called "watermelon" in Spanish. Imagine drinking your morning coffee on a portal (New Mexican for "porch") while watching the sun rise and the mountains turn pink. In other Southwestern states, similar views cost a lot of money, but in New Mexico, you can see this every day for surprisingly low prices. In towns like Las Cruces, Silver City, and Truth or Consequences, retirees can find homes with views of the mountains or desert that would cost three times as much in nearby states.

New Mexico is truly unique because of its rich cultural tapestry, which is made up of Native American, Hispanic, and English influences that go back hundreds of years. This is not fake tourism; it's real history that makes everyday life better. On the weekends, you could visit old pueblo homes, shop at real Native American markets, or take part in festivals that have been going on for hundreds of years. The state's three-cultural heritage isn't just a catchphrase; it's a way of life that makes retirement more interesting and full.

The natural beauty of New Mexico is hard to explain. Other states might have deserts or mountains, but New Mexico has an amazing range of landscapes that are all very easy to get to. There are times when you can hike through red rock canyons, mountains covered in pine trees, and the Bosque del Apache, where you can watch birds migrate. The diversity of environments means retirees never run out of new places to explore, and the state's relatively low population means you can often have these spectacular settings almost to yourself.

But for middle-class retirees, New Mexico isn't just about the scenery and culture; it's also about the freedom that comes with a lower cost of living. When you retire and your basic expenses use up less of your income, life opens up in ways you didn't expect. This raises an interesting question: How do you maximize the unique opportunities New Mexico offers while maintaining a comfortable retirement budget?

Key Things to Think About

It's not what many retirees would expect when it comes to health care in New Mexico. There are some modern hospitals in the state, especially in Albuquerque and Santa Fe. But what makes it unique is how it combines traditional and alternative medicine. Because the state has a long history of healing traditions, it has a unique medical landscape where traditional Native American and Hispanic healing practices coexist with modern medicine. A lot of retirees find this all-around approach very helpful, especially when it comes to dealing with long-term conditions.

The state's medical infrastructure keeps changing and growing. More and more telemedicine programs are helping people in rural areas get the care they need. Big hospitals like the University of New Mexico Hospital offer cutting-edge care, and smaller hospitals in rural areas make sure that everyone in the state can get the basic care they need. For retirees who are thinking about moving to a less populated area, it's important to know that many communities in New Mexico have come up with creative ways to make healthcare more accessible, such as regular visiting specialist clinics and medical transport services.

Seniors moving from states with higher housing costs will find housing options in New Mexico that almost seem too good to be true. With their thick walls and natural insulation, adobe homes are not only cute, but they're also good for the environment, keeping your utility bills low in hot summers and cool winters. Retirees often find that they can afford custom homes with mountain views in cities like Las Cruces or Alamogordo. Even in more popular areas, like the edges of Santa Fe, housing prices are still low compared to other places with similar artistic communities.

The cost benefits go far beyond housing. New Mexico has some of the lowest property taxes in the country, and the state has a lot of tax breaks for retirees. Most of the time, grocery bills are lower than the national average. This is especially true if you buy local and seasonal foods. Many retirees find that their Social Security checks go further here, which lets them live a more comfortable life than they could in coastal states.

New Mexico has its own unique rhythm to daily life. The pace is slow, but it's never dull. Local farmers' markets are great places to get fresh food and meet new people. From art walks to chili festivals, community events offer regular entertainment that doesn't break the bank for retirees. Many retirees become interested in photography or painting because of the state's famously light and clear air. Others are drawn to pottery, weaving, or other traditional crafts taught by local artists.

People who live in New Mexico should pay extra attention to the outdoor lifestyle they can enjoy all year long. In contrast to states with extreme weather, New Mexico's climate lets people enjoy the outdoors all year long. Different elevations across the state let you get away from the heat in the summer in mountain towns or find warmth in the winter in southern towns. Hiking trails are rarely crowded, whether you're going for an easy walk or a difficult trek. Golf courses in this state have beautiful views without the high prices you'd find in other Southwestern states.

The intellectual life in New Mexico may surprise people who are new here the most. Two national laboratories, Los Alamos and Sandia, make it possible for people to keep learning throughout their lives. There are free or low-cost lectures, concerts, and cultural events in places like Las Cruces and Socorro that are home to major universities. Many retirees keep their minds sharp by taking college classes on the side or joining discussion groups. This also helps them meet new people.

There are artist communities all over the state that make retirement even more enjoyable. Even though Santa Fe's galleries are well-known, Silver City, Madrid, and Taos also have lively art scenes and more affordable living costs. The state's beautiful light and landscapes inspire many retirees to find their own creative skills. Art classes, workshops, and cooperative galleries are all great ways to learn new things and meet new people.

New Mexico's rich cultural diversity makes it a great place to grow as a person and get involved in your community.

There are festivals in the area that honor a wide range of topics, from Native

American traditions to the history of the Spanish colonies to modern art. Unlike other events that are geared toward tourists, these celebrations are real expressions of cultures that are still alive. Retirees often find themselves welcomed into these traditions, learning new customs and perspectives that enrich their retirement years.

The magic of New Mexico retirement reveals itself slowly, like a desert sunrise gradually illuminating the landscape. Ruth and Bobby Fernandez moved from Oregon three years ago. Ruth says, "Our friends thought we were making a strange choice." "Now they visit and understand. Everything about this place is healing, from the weather to the way people live. We're living better on less, and our retirement feels richer than we ever imagined."

The Fernandez family and others have found that New Mexico offers something that is becoming harder to find in today's world: a chance to get off the typical retirement treadmill and into something more real. Success here isn't measured by having a country club membership or a dealership for expensive cars. Instead, it's in the beauty of the sunrise, the strength of your community ties, and the freedom to discover interests you didn't know you had.

The math behind how much it costs to live in New Mexico often surprises people who are new here in a good way. When your home costs half as much as it would in California or Colorado, your property taxes are some of the lowest in the country, and solar panels lower your utility bills, all of a sudden, your retirement budget gives you more options. When people retire, they often have extra money that they can use for hobbies, travel, or just enjoying life without having to worry about money all the time.

For those intrigued by New Mexico's possibilities, consider this approach: visit during different seasons, but don't just be a tourist. Spend time in local coffee shops where people naturally speak both English and Spanish. If you are invited, go to a pueblo feast day. Visit small towns like Truth or

Consequences, which has both hot springs and art galleries. Notice how the mountains' light changes as the day goes on. Let the state's rhythm sync with your own.

Don't just look at the well-known spots. There's no denying that Santa Fe is beautiful, but towns like Silver City, Ruidoso, and Las Cruces also have beautiful things to offer at prices that are more reasonable. New Mexico has a lot of different places to live, from mountain retreats to desert oasis, from artist colonies to college towns, so retirees can find the perfect place for them.

New Mexico retirement looks especially good for people from the middle class. As working from home becomes more common, small towns are getting better infrastructure and new amenities. As healthcare networks continue to grow, they make it easier for people in rural areas to get medical care. The state's dedication to clean energy sources helps keep living costs stable, and its efforts to save water help make sure it will be around for a long time.

The beauty of New Mexico retirement is that it's not for everyone. It's for people who like dirt roads and adobe walls. This is for people who value real experiences over fake comforts. It's for retired people who know that real luxury isn't about keeping up with the Joneses but about being able to live your own life.

```
Remember that picking New Mexico as your retirement spot isn't
about going with the flow; it's about being smart enough to know
that the best retirement spots are sometimes hidden from view.
While most retirees are going to more typical places, smart ones
are finding that the Land of Enchantment is a great place to go
because it is both affordable and real.
```

New Mexico is known as the Land of Enchantment for a reason. It's a place where time moves a little differently, where ancient traditions blend seamlessly with modern life, and where middle-class retirees can still afford to chase their dreams. New Mexico has a lot to offer, whether you're looking for a rich cultural life, exciting outdoor activities, artistic inspiration, or just the freedom to retire without worrying about money.

It's possible that the state motto, "Crescit eundo" (it grows as it goes), could be used to describe retirement in this area. Many people find that their retirement dreams don't just live on in New Mexico; they grow and take on new forms they never thought possible. Maybe that's what makes New Mexico so magical—not just its beautiful scenery or rich history, but also its power to make you rethink what retirement can be.

Making Your Middle-Class Retirement Dream a Reality

As we've journeyed through these seven remarkable states, each offering its own unique blend of advantages for middle-class retirees, one truth becomes crystal clear: affordable, high-quality retirement isn't just possible – it's abundantly available if you know where to look. Let's weave together the insights we've gathered and create a practical framework for your decision-making process.

The State-by-State Advantage Matrix

Each of our featured states offers distinct benefits that appeal to different retirement priorities:

Florida dazzles with its tax benefits and established retirement infrastructure, but its true value lies in the lesser-known communities away from costly coastal areas. For middle-class retirees, the central and northern regions offer all the sunshine without the premium price tag.

Tennessee emerges as a financial powerhouse, combining no state income tax with low property taxes and a moderate cost of living. Its diverse geography, from the music-filled streets of Nashville to the serenity of the Smoky Mountains, provides options for every lifestyle preference.

Michigan surprises with its combination of natural beauty and economic value. The Great Lakes State offers affordable waterfront living opportunities that would be unthinkable on either coast, along with distinct seasons that keep life interesting and engaging.

Arizona demonstrates that desert living doesn't require a fortune. While others flock to Scottsdale and Paradise Valley, savvy retirees are discovering charming communities with the same climate advantages and modern amenities at fraction of the cost.

Delaware proves that East Coast retirement doesn't have to drain your savings. Its strategic location and tax advantages create opportunities for retirees to maintain their Northeast connections while stretching their retirement dollars significantly further.

South Carolina blends Southern charm with geographic diversity, offering everything from mountain towns to coastal communities at reasonable prices. Its growing healthcare infrastructure and cultural scene make it increasingly attractive for middle-class retirees.

New Mexico rounds out our list by offering something increasingly rare – authenticity combined with affordability. The Land of Enchantment provides cultural richness and stunning landscapes without requiring a fortune to enjoy them.

Future Trends Reshaping Retirement Migration

Looking ahead, several key trends are reshaping retirement migration patterns in ways that favor middle-class retirees:

Remote healthcare services are expanding, making it easier to choose locations based on lifestyle preferences rather than proximity to major medical centers. Telemedicine and visiting specialist programs are making healthcare more accessible in smaller communities.

Climate change considerations are shifting traditional retirement patterns. States like Michigan and Tennessee are gaining appeal as mild havens, while traditional retirement states face increasing environmental challenges.

Technology infrastructure is becoming more uniformly available, enabling retirees to maintain connections with family and access services from virtually anywhere. This democratization of technology is opening up previously overlooked locations as viable retirement destinations.

Small and mid-sized cities are experiencing cultural renaissances, offering the amenities of larger cities without the corresponding costs. This trend is creating new pockets of opportunity for middle-class retirees in all seven states.

A Framework for Making Your Choice

As you evaluate these destinations, consider this practical decision-making framework:

1. Financial Foundation

- Calculate your monthly retirement income
- Research state-specific tax implications
- Compare housing costs in different regions
- Investigate insurance costs, particularly in coastal areas
- Consider future cost-of-living trends

2. Lifestyle Alignment

- Define your non-negotiable quality of life factors
- Evaluate climate preferences honestly
- Consider proximity to family and friends
- Assess cultural and recreational priorities
- Think about your ideal community size

3. Healthcare Considerations

- Map out existing health conditions and specialist needs
- Research healthcare infrastructure in potential areas
- Consider future medical needs and accessibility
- Evaluate insurance networks and coverage

4. Long-term Sustainability

- Think about aging in place
- Consider community walkability
- Evaluate public transportation options
- Assess future development plans in potential areas

Making the Final Choice

Remember, the perfect retirement destination combines financial sustainability with personal fulfillment. Here are some final considerations:

- **Visit potential locations during different seasons**

- Rent before buying to test your choice
- Connect with local retiree groups
- Research property appreciation trends
- Consider proximity to major airports for family visits
- Evaluate part-time work opportunities if desired

The beauty of these seven states lies in their ability to accommodate different versions of the retirement dream while respecting middle-class budgets. Whether you're drawn to desert sunsets or ocean breezes, mountain trails or cultural events, there's a place where your retirement dreams can flourish without compromising your financial security.

Your ideal retirement destination might not be the most famous or the most expensive – but it will be the one that lets you live your best life within your means. After all, the true measure of retirement success isn't how much you spend, but how richly you live.

> The journey to finding your perfect retirement home starts with understanding your options and ends with making an informed choice that aligns with both your dreams and your resources. These seven states offer proof that middle-class retirement can be not just comfortable, but truly extraordinary.